The Best 30 Things To Do In London

An Experienced Traveler's Guide To The Best Tourist Attractions and Hotspots within London

Jon Steel

ISBN: 9781798822937

CONTENTS

INTRODUCTION

Welcome to "30 Things To Do In London," by Jon Steel. This handy guide is a perfect companion for any traveler wanting to gain an in-depth knowledge of the top 30 tourist attractions, Hotspots, points of interests and things to do within London. London is the capital city of the United Kingdom and is among one of the world's oldest cities, with a history that spans nearly two millennia! London is by far the largest metropolis in Britain and is also the country's economic, transportation and cultural center. London is also one of the most popular tourist and business destinations in the entire world and over 17 million unique visitors flock to London each year! This manual covers everything from where to eat and shop to where to stay and explore! No two cities are the same! Each location has its own history, culture and vibe! We highly recommended supplementing the suggested activities, within this guide, with recommendations from locals! Ask the staff at the hotels you are staying in, ask a waiter in a restaurant, ask a newspaper seller on the street – locals will all have an invaluable insight into their home city! It's important to note that the 30 things listed within this book are based on the experiences and collective opinions of the Jon Steel family. We hope that this guide helps you to optimize your holiday time in old London Town! Have a wonderful holiday!

1. LONDON EYE

The London Eye was originally designed and commissioned to mark the turning of the millennium. Since its construction, the London Eye has established itself as one the most iconic aspects of the London skyline. The giant Ferris Wheel began turning in the spring of 2000 and is actually the world's tallest cantilevered observation wheel. The Eye has pods, that have a space-age aesthetic, which carry visitors slowly to a peak height of 135 meters which gives stunning views of Big Ben, the Thames river, the Shard and many of central London's other landmarks. Each pod is surprisingly large and can hold up to 25 passengers! The experience starts off with a brief 4D film in County Hall when you go to pick up your tickets. You will then need to queue for your turn to enter one of the many pods – the queue is generally fast moving but can take a long period of time during the summer holidays due to an increase in visitors. The pod takes around thirty minutes to make a full rotation and the ride feels steady and smooth. The London Eye's pods are wheelchair accessible and staff are happy to help accommodate any customer who may need assistance boarding.

Price

A general admissions ticket for one rotation of the London Eye costs £26 for adults, £21 for children between the ages of 3 and 15. Children under 3 can board the Eye for free. It is important to note that purchasing a ticket on the day is more expensive than booking in advance online. The London Eye also has multiple different offers such as the 'Day & Night' deal, which allows customers to take two trips on the Eye (once during the day and once after dark) for a price of £32.45.

Location

Riverside Building, Country Hall, SE1 7PB

2. THE SHARD

The Shard's construction was completed in 2012 and it is currently the tallest tower in London's skyline. The Shard was designed by an Italian architect called Renzo Plano. Plano was inspired by the spires he'd seen in the eighteenth-century London landscapes painted by Canaletto. The tower is truly a multipurpose building as it houses offices, a hotel, restaurants and residences. The Shard's inhabitable floors make up 'The View from The Shard' observatory. The observatory offers a stunning 244 meter high 360-degree view of London. Since opening to the public in the early months of 2013, the building has also often been used for many interesting events such as silent discos, yoga and banquets. On your trip to London you will always be able to visit the Shard as it is open 7 days a week, 364 days a year. A visit to the observatory starts on the ground floor where you step into a kaleidoscopic lift that travels at high speeds to the viewing platform. The observatory has floor-to-ceiling windows which allows everyone, big and small, to experience the amazing panoramic view. The Shard offers views of all of London's most iconic landmarks that lie within a 40 mile radius of the building. The viewing platform is located on the 68th floor and spans over three spacious levels. The building also has an open air Skydeck that is located on its 72nd floor. The

Skydeck offer visitors a chance to use specially designed touchscreen telescopes to see the surrounding sights in much greater detail, while also being provided with onscreen information about them! The telescopes provide information in 10 different languages in an aim to be as inclusive as possible. Throughout the year, the Shard hosts a wide range of special installations. The most popular of these have been the summer garden, which is made up of over 2,000 wild flowers and plants, and the winter wonderland, which was created by the gastro-wizards Bompass & Parr. Every Sunday a team from the Museum of London set up a free exhibition in the Shard, known as 'Objects in Focus,' which allows visitors to handle objects from their extensive collection which includes items discovered from the archaeological dig at the 2012 Olympic site. The 'Objects in Focus' sessions run from 10:30am to 4pm and are free to all ticket-holding visitors.

Price

A general ticket of admission to the Shard costs £25.95 for a student, £24.95 for a child between the ages of 4 and 15, £26.95 for a disabled adult (which includes entry for a carer), £23.95 for a disabled child (which includes entry for a carer) and £26.95 for an adult. It is important to note that you can book your tickets online and save £5!

Location

Joiner St, SE1 9QU

3. BRITISH MUSEUM

1759 saw the opening of London's 'British Museum,' which was also the first national museum to be open to the public in the entire world! Admittance to the museum was free for the purpose of providing 'studious and curious persons' a place to explore and learn – luckily for you, admittance to the 'British Museum' is still free! Centuries before the internet or television, the 'British Museum' allowed the general population to examine and learn about antiques and objects of cultural importance from all around the globe. This helped fuel London's connection to, love of and acceptance of other cultures, both ancient and contemporary. The first ever exhibition consisted of a collection of coins, medals, books and natural remains and was given to the 'British Museum' by a physician known as Sir Hans Sloane. Ever since then the 'British Museum' has become the home to many of the most significant finds made by British explorers, archeologists and historians. Two of the most interesting exhibitions include the Rosetta Stone (which was created in Ancient Egypt) and the Parthenon sculpture (which is from Acropolis in Athens). In recent years there have been much debate about whether the 'British Museum' should return some of their historic treasures to the countries they originated from – for example a campaign has recently been started by the Greek government to determine who has the legal rights to the Elgin Marbles. The 'British Museum' has over 6million visitors a year – which makes it one of London's most popular tourist attractions – and we highly suggest that you also check it out on your visit to London! To experience the full extent of what the 'British Museum' has to offer, we recommend signing up to a tour (either via tour guide or audio tour guide). A guided tour will allow you to fully embrace the history and any other interesting facts behind each piece. It is worth noting that guided tours are free on Fridays!

Price

There is no fee of admission to the 'British Museum.'

Location

44 Great Russel St, WC1B 3DG

4. EMIRATES AIR LINE

The Emirates Air Line is situated in east London and can be found by the Excel Centre on the north side of the river and by the O2 Arena on the south side of the river. The Emirates Air Line is the UK's first urban cable car system. The ride will take you across the 1.1km stretch between the landing points at a relatively fast pace – the cable car system is capable of transporting over 2,500 people per hour in each direction! While crossing the river, passengers will have an amazing view of the City, Canary Wharf, the Thames Barrier and the Olympic Park. We recommended taking the Emirates Air Line at night as the view is enhanced by all of London's lights! During the summer a service called 'Night Flights' is available, which offers a much longer journey time as well as audio and visual entertainment. The Emirates Air Line is easily accessible as admission can be bought using an Oyster card or a contactless credit/debit card. If you are using an Oyster card it is important to note that a trip on the Emirates Air Line is not included in the daily spend capping.

Price

A one way trip on the Emirates Air Line will cost £1.70 for a child and £3.50 for an adult if you use an

Oyster card or a contactless card. If you buy a ticket from the ticket office it will cost £2.30 for children and £4.50 for adults.

Location

27 Western Gateway, E16 4FA

5. KEW GARDENS

The Royal Botanic Gardens, commonly referred to as simply 'Kew Gardens', at Kew are over 250 years old and are still a highly popular tourist attraction in modern times. One of Kew Gardens biggest attractions is its 'Victorian Palm House,' which houses multiple different species of large plants. The 'Victorian Palm House' was developed during the reign of George III and is one of two national bases for research and education into the field of botanical studies. Scientists will be tending to, and studying, the plants while you explore the giant green houses. We recommend looking out for the giant, stinking Titan Arum, which is located in the Princess of Wales Conservatory, as it is truly a luscious and intriguing specimen. Kew Gardens is also home to England's oldest surviving Victorian greenhouse, known as the Temperate House. Kew's greenhouses are designed and maintained to nurture the plants in an environment which allows them to fully thrive. If you are unfazed by heights, we recommend climbing up to the Tree Top Walkway which stands at 18 meters tall. While the Walkway might be windy on occasions, it gives a completely different perspective on the beautiful gardens and plants. Many people visit Kew Gardens for artistic inspiration as there is such a wide variety of plant life, which all receives incredible up keeping. The

Gardens are also full of floral sculptures which change with the season, for example the 'Reclining Mother and Child' by Henry Moore. Kew Gardens updates their website on a weekly basis with a section called 'What to See this Week.' This constantly updated section is the best way to find out what shows, exhibitions and other activities are available to you! If you are a lover of plants, flowers and strolling through beautiful landscapes we would highly recommend visit Kew Gardens.

Price

The price on entry to Kew Gardens will cost £3.50 for a child between the age of 4-16 and £14 for adults. There are a wide range of deals available – such as a family pass which can cost anywhere between £19 and £34.

Location

Royal Botanic Gardens, TW98 3AB

6. NATURAL HISTORY MUSEUM

The National History Museum is a mixture of a top level academic research facility and also a fabulously intriguing museum that is open to the public. The Museum opened in 1881 in Alfred Waterhouse's purpose-built Romanesque cathedral of nature on Cromwell Road. An extension, called the Darwin Centre, was added in 2009. The Museum is a feat of architectural brilliance and its beautiful pale blue terracotta façade gives a good indication of the beauty of the treasures found within the Museum. Arguably the Museum's most famous piece is Dippy the Diplodocus, which has resided in the Hintze Hall since 1905. Dippy is a 26 meter long plaster-cast replica of a Diplodocus skeleton. Dippy goes on many tours around the United Kingdom and most recently made an appearance on Dorset's Jurassic Coast. While Dippy is away there is a huge Blue Whale skeleton taking up his spot. The Museum's west wing is known as the 'Blue Zone.' The 'Blue Zone' has a plethora of animatronic dinosaurs, displays on biology, a man-sized model of a human fetus in the womb and graphic diagrams. The Museum's east wing is known as the 'Green Zone.' The 'Green Zone' includes a giant cross-section of a Giant Sequoia tree, an amazing array of stuffed birds (including the extinct Dodo) and a huge collection of bird eggs. The

Hummingbird egg is as a small as a little fingernail which is amazing when contrasted to the football-sized eggs of the Elephant bird. If you head north from the entrance you will find yourself in the 'Red Zone.' The 'Red Zone' allows visitors to take an escalator through the center of the Earth and is also home to the popular earthquake simulator. Each year the Museum features fresh and exciting temporary exhibitions to compliment the consistent wonders of the stationary exhibitions. If you have an interest in natural history or just love exploring amazing exhibitions – the Natural History Museum will surely not disappoint! To experience the full extent of what the Natural History Museum has to offer, we recommend signing up to a tour (either via tour guide or audio tour guide). A guided tour will allow you to fully embrace the history and any other interesting facts behind each piece.

Price

The Natural History Museum is free of charge to enter. Some temporary exhibitions will have a price of entry however.

Location

Cromwell Road, SW7 5BD

7. BIG BEN

Big Ben is one of the world's most famous and celebrated clocks. The name 'Big Ben' refers to the clock's bell, while the tower is known as the 'Clock Tower' or 'St Stephen's Tower.' Big Ben was designed by architect Charles Barry as part of the Palace of Westminster and the Clock Tower was completed in 1859. The huge clock started on the 31st of May on the year of its completion and the main bell first chimed on the 11th of July. The quarter bell did not chime for the first time until the 7th of September. The clock is surprisingly accurate thanks to its counterweight system which is made up of old pennies. Traditionally the national time, within the United Kingdom, is based upon the time kept by Big Ben. UK residents can arrange a tour of the Clock Tower through their local MP or a member of the House of Lords. While the Clock Tower itself isn't open to foreign visitors, the base of Big Ben is crowded with information booths, souvenir vendors and tourists taking photos.

Price

There is no price of admission to Big Ben.

Location

Westminster, SW1A 0AA

8. THE RITZ

While the Ritz may not be the best hotel for you to spend the entirety of your trip at, as standard rooms cost between £300 and £1000, it is definitely worth staying for a single night or at least visiting the building. If you can afford to spend a night at the Ritz, we highly recommend it as there are no hotels like it in all of London and it offers a truly unique experience. The Ritz hotel has been setting the bar for luxury ever since it opened in 1906, so doing things on a budget is not really the point of the Ritz experience. The building is full of sparkling crystal chandeliers, marble plinths, mirrored walls, lush carpets and beautifully upholstered furniture. There is even an in-house gilder who traverses the building and makes sure that all of the gold leaf keeps on gleaming! The swanky hotel sits relatively close to other swanky London locations such as the Wolseley, Buckingham Palace and Fortnum & Mason. Each room has a huge and cozy bed that will make it difficult for any visitor to leave their room. Each room also comes with a fresh and thick dressing gown that is embossed with the Ritz's regal logo. Everything about the Ritz is extravagant: even the bathrooms have gilded golden taps and marble toilets. Some visitors are known to find the grandeur of the Ritz slightly overwhelming at first. The building also has a lack of modern technology as it has attempted to keep the experience it offers as traditional as possible. Visitors flock to the Ritz for its heritage and traditional style which creates an heir of grandeur and occasion during any stay. The Ritz is as close to traditional perfection as you are every likely to experience.

Price

A room at the Ritz can cost anywhere between £300-£1000/per night for a standard room. However the Ritz also offers more upscale suites that can exceed £1000!

Location

150 Piccadilly, W1J 9BR

9. THAMES ROCKETS

The Thames Rockets are a fleet of click RIBs (ridged inflatable boats) which offer a thrilling, high-speed boat ride along the Thames. You can acquire a ticket for a ride on the phone, online or at the Millennium Pier (which is located near to the London Eye). It is important to arrive 20 minutes before your RIB is set to leave as you will need to be kitted out with a life jacket, a waterproof jacket and a goggle-style visor. The trip will start off relatively slowly and calmly as the guide entertains the customers with fun facts and tidbits about London, a breakdown the sights and amusing celebrity stories. However, once the RIB passes Tower Bridge it will REALLY speed up. The RIB will zigzag excitingly down the Thames until it reaches Canary Wharf where it turns around and speeds back to the base camp. The Thames Rockets are a great way to experience the sights of London from a completely unique perspective. The Rockets reach speeds of up to 30 knots and will vastly outpace the slower sightseeing cruises.

Price

A seat on a Thames Rocket will cost £25.95 for children under the age of 14 and £43.50 for an adult.

Location

Boarding Gate One, London Eye Millennium Pier, SE1 7PB

10. BRIGIT'S BAKERY

Amidst the hustle and bustle of the modern Covent Garden is a small little tea room known as 'Brigit's Bakery.' The former famous BB Bakery, located in Covent Garden, has recently had a largescale makeover and has rebranded itself as the Brigit's Bakery. Brigit's Bakery is the perfect place to sit and enjoy a coffee, afternoon tea, a cake or two, and lunch. The business was originally set up by Brigitte Bloch and her son Cedric, who wanted to provide Londoners and visitors with traditional English tea time pastries for a relatively low price. The bakery specializes in Afternoon Tea with a somewhat French Twist that we are sure any customer would appreciate and adore. Brigit's Bakery offers private rooms and a large amount of downstairs seating which allows customers to truly remove themselves from the busy streets of London. While all the pastries and cakes are of a heavily quality, we would highly recommend the lemon meringue tart as it is truly divine and a favorite amongst frequent visitors!

Price

The price of pastries is highly varied on which pastry you wish to purchase.

Location

6-7 Chandos Place, Covent Garden, WC2N 4HU

11.TATE MODERN

The Tate Modern's industrial architecture leaves most people in utter awe before they have even had a chance to view the contents of the art gallery. The Tate was built after World War II and was designed by Sir Giles Gilbert Scott. Interestingly the Tate Modern was originally designed to serve as a power station for Battersea however the building was converted into an art gallery in 1981, a mere 20 years after its construction. Ever since the Tate Modern opened its door as an art gallery and art museum it has been incredibly popular amongst both locals and visitors. The gallery attracts over 5million visitors a year! The original building was not a suitable size to deal with such high traffic of visitors, so the first extension was built. The TM2 extension cost roughly £250,000,000 and opened in 2012! The extension is mainly used to house stage performances and film based art. A further origami style extension, designed by Herzog & de Meuron, was opened in the later part of 2016. The main galleries are cavernous in size and hold countless original and permanent art installations from the 1900s onwards. The permanent collection is highly revered as being one of the best curated collections in the world and features Matisse, Rothko and Beuys. However the main draw to the Tate Modern is its large-scale, temporary instillations which change on a regular basis. To experience the full extent of what the Tate Modern has to offer, we recommend signing up to a tour (either via tour guide or audio tour guide). A guided tour will allow you to fully embrace the history and any other interesting facts behind each piece. If you have a love of modern art, fantastic architecture and culture we highly recommend visiting the Tate Modern.

Price

Access the Tate Modern's permanent collection is free of charge. Some of the temporary instillations may charge a premium – but the premium price will be dependent on the insulation itself.

Location

Bankside, SE1 9TG

12.WESTMINSTER ABBEY

Westminster Abbey is the epitome of gothic architectural grandeur and has been the site of 16 royal weddings, countless important funerals and every single royal coronation since 1066. Westminster Abbey allows visitors to peruse the graves, tablets, busts, stone dedications and historical artifacts related to England's monarchy over the last century. The Abbey itself is the burial site of seventeen English Kings and Queens, along with countless dukes, countesses and figure of historical importance – such as Behn, Darwin, Dickens, Hardy and Olivier. There are over 3,000 souls honored throughout the chapels and cloisters within the Abbey. There is also a huge and intricate stained glass window which is dedicated to Isambard Kingdom Brunel. The 'Poet's Conner' is situated in the Abbey's South Transept and pays homage to the United Kingdom's most celebrated writers such as Jane Austen, William Shakespeare, William Blake and Sir John Betjeman. There are multiple different areas that are accessible for visit in the Abbey itself and the Abbey's gardens. Sadly the Abbey's museum is closed until mid-2018 as it is going through a refurbishment process. It is important to remember that the Westminster Abbey is a fully functioning church which means that visiting times can vary. It is recommend to check the website for visiting times before actually visiting the church itself. The website will also outline the times available for visitors to take guided tours around the Abbey. There are free organ recitals every Sunday at 5:45pm.

Price

Visiting the Abbey will cost £9 for children under the age of 17 and £20 for adults.

Location

Broad Sanctuary, 20 Deans Yd, SW1P 3PA

13. HELICOPTER FLIGHT

There are few sights better than a bird's eye view of a bustling city. London has a plethora of incredible landmarks that are scattered around in every direction – it would be almost impossible to visit them all in a short stay in London. However a quick flight in a helicopter will allow you to view of the sights from a truly unique perspective. Gaze at the beauty of the Thames as it winds its way through one of the world's busiest cities and marvel at the unique and interesting skyline found in London. In Battersea there are two helicopter flight packages available: 12 minuet flights and 18 minuet flights. Both flights allow for amazing aerial views as it follows the Thames down towards Buckingham Palace, Big Ben, Houses of Parliament and many many more landmarks. The helicopters seat a maximum of six passengers and takes off and touches down in Battersea, Central London.

Price

The price of a 12 minuet flight is £150 per head. The price of a 18 minuet flight is £220 per head. It is important to note that helicopter flights depart between 12pm and 5pm.

Location

Battersea, London

14. BRIXTON WINDMILL

The Brixton Windmill was constructed in 1816 and was in service until the mid-1930s. The Windmill reopened to the public in 2011 after going over £500,000 worth of reconstruction and restoration. The Windmill has recently been shortlisted for a Museums and Heritage Award for Excellence. It is important for all visitors to note that as a former industrial building, the Windmill has multiple potentially dangerous areas and all visitors should abide by the safety precautions. Some of the potential dangers include heavy machinery, low support beams and high ladders. The Windmill holds open days periodically throughout the year and it is advisable for visitors to check dates and availability online before visiting the Windmill. The inside of the Windmill is relatively small which means that there can only be a very limited number of visitors at any given time. Children are welcome to explore the first floor of the Windmill but are not allowed to climb the steep ladders as a safety precaution. On open days there are short tours, which do not require booking, of the building and an explanation of the buildings history and importance to the local area. It is possible to book full guided tours which explore all of the floors of the building – these must be booked in advance and online.

Price

Open days include March 30th and 31st, April 13th and 14th, May 6th, 11th and 12th, June 8th, 9th, 22nd and 23rd, July 27th – August 4th, August 10th and 11th, September 14, 15th and 22nd and October 5th, 12th and 13th. The guided tours cost a premium that it is dependent on the amount of bookings.

Location

Windmill Gardens, West end of Blenheim Gardens, SW2 5EU

15. MADAME TUSSAUDS

Madame Tussauds was originally a European art exhibition that came into existence during the 18th century. Madame Tussauds herself began the tradition be immortalizing figures from the bloody French Revolution. The first Madame Tussauds Museum was open on Baker Street in London where she presented figures who were involved in sensational crimes across Europe and the world. Now, over 150 years since the death of Madame Tussauds, her legacy still lives on through the figures within the museums located in several major cities around the world, with London and New York being two of the most popular. The Madam Tussauds located on Marylebone Road is undoubtedly one of the most popular of the museums. The figures within the London collection include various movie stars, singers, athletes, politicians and other figures of historical importance. Madam Tussauds is a popular tourist attraction for the young and pop culturally obsessed as most of the figures pertain to modern, and current, history. Each model is hand made by a team of artists, who use photographs, precise measurements, casts and oil paints. It is estimated that each figure costs over £200,000 to create! Tussauds also is home to the Marvel Super Heroes 4D interactives and waxworks of Iron Man, Spiderman and a giant 18 foot tall Hulk! If you are a Marvel fan then Tussauds is a must visit for you as it allows for some really unique photo opportunities. The Marvel exhibition also offers a 9minuet 4D film which includes real effects such as smoke and ground tremors. There is also a very impressive Star Wars exhibition which includes the swamps of Dagobah, the Millenium Falcon and a plethora of Lucasfilms Ltd approved characters including: Han Solo, Princess Leia and Chewbacca!

Price

A ticket of admission to Madam Tussauds is £28.80 for children and £33 for adults. It is important to note that tickets are normally between £5-£10 cheaper if you book online!

Location

Marylebone Rd, NW1 5LR

16. THE GUILDHALL ART GALLERY

London's Guildhall Art Gallery mainly focuses on art produced in the nineteenth century – specifically painting produced by Leighton, Constable, Millais, Rossetti, Holman and Hunt, to name by a few. If you venture to the downstairs exhibitions there are paintings of London which have been produced all the way from the mid-1660s to the present day. This exhibition gives visitors an incredible insight into how London has changed throughout the centuries. The paintings include depictions of war, melancholy workers on the streets during the depression and a detailed plan of George Dance's never constructed London Bridge replacement. The collection's center piece is the massive 'Siege of Gibraltar' which was produce by John Copley. This huge painting spans two entire floors of the purpose built gallery! The Gallery also includes a sub-basement which contains the remains of London's 6,000-seater Roman-style amphitheater which was constructed around AD70. The Gallery also houses multiple temporary exhibitions which add a further level of uniqueness to his gallery. If you are looking to explore a truly unique and mixed collection of art work, then look no further than the Guildhall Art Gallery.

Price

A ticket of entry to the permanent collections of art costs £3. To explore all of the temporary exhibitions it will cost an extra £2 (so £5 to view the whole of the gallery).

Location

Guildhall Yard, off Gresham St, EC2V 5AE

17. TOWER BRIDGE

No visit to London is complete without crossing its iconic Tower Bridge. Despite being one of the most famous river crossings in the world, Tower Bridge is actually only a mere 123 years old! The huge bridge is capable of raising itself in the middle to allow large vessels to pass underneath - which makes it a truly impressive piece of engineering. The Bridge has been a part of multiple iconic moments: planes have flown through it, David Beckham has steered a powerboat underneath it and in 1952 a double-decker bus, full of passengers, flew over the gap between the two halves of the bridge as they began to raise without warning! When Tower Bridge was first constructed, in 1894, it was powered by steam and was considered to be the pinnacle of Victorian engineering. The Bridge went through a modernization process in 1974. The modernization process included the installation of electro-hydraulic systems which allowed Tower Bridge's raising mechanism to be vastly more reliable and safe. It is still possible to see all of the Bridge's old steam engines, inside the base of the towers, with a ticket to the Tower Bridge Experience. The Tower Bridge Experience also allows entry to the overhead walkways which offer some of the most beautiful views of London, the Thames and the road situated on the bridge itself. In

2014, the Bridge's 120th birthday, a 11 meter glass floor was placed on the upper walkway which allows visitors to stand, and gaze down, a whopping 42 meters! A ticket to the Tower Bridge Experience also offers visitors a chance to explore the Bridge's exhibition which honors the marvelous feat of engineering present in global bridge design, as well as entry to an art installation. If you are booking a ticket to walk across the Bridge's walkways it is important to note that the bridge does raise unexpected based on the movement of registered ships. On average the bridge raises 850 times a year!

Price

Crossing the bridge in a vehicle is free of charge. A ticket to the Tower Bridge Experience costs £9 for adults, £3.90 for children under the age of 16 and £6.30 for students. It is important to note that ticket prices are discounted if purchased online.

Location

Tower Bridge, Tower Bridge Rd, SE1 2UP

18.HOUSES OF PARLIAMENT

The Houses of Parliament is the political epicenter of the United Kingdom. Parliament itself is housed in the Thames-side Palace of Westminster and is situated directly by Big Ben. There are tours of Parliament available which offer an insight into thousands of years of history, modern day politics and the political system in place within the United Kingdom. The guided tours will also give visitors a chance to view the amazing art and architecture present within the Houses of Parliament. There is also an audio tour which brings to life the mechanics behind the House of Lords and the House of Commons. The audio tour lasts for around 75 minutes and features leading Parliamentary figures such as the Speaker and Black Rod. The majority of places visited on the tours were built in the mid-19th century due to a devastating fire, which occurred in 1834, that destroy much of the original parliamentary building. However the tours also include a walk through the stunning Westminster Hall which dates back as far as 1097. The other points of interest that you will visit during a tour are the Royal Gallery, the Queen's Robing Room, the Central Lobby, the Lords Chamber and the Commons Chamber – which is where the majority of debates are held.

Price

A guided tour will cost £18 for adults, £15.50 for students and £7.20 for children under the age of 16. It is important to note that audio tours normally cost dramatically less than guided tours – as guided tours are much more popular. If you are a UK resident, it is possible to have a full tour of the Houses of Parliament by contacting your local MP or member of the House of Lords.

Location

Palace of Westminster, SW1A 0AA

19.ST PAUL'S CATHEDRAL

St Paul's Cathedral, which was designed by Christopher Wren, is truly an architectural masterpiece and one of London's most beautiful landmarks. St Paul's Cathedral was constructed after its predecessor burnt down during the Great Fire of London which occurred in 1666. During World War II most of the churches within central London were completely destroyed, however St Paul's Cathedral completely survived the devastation of the Blitz. After the conclusion of the War, St Paul's was also the place that Londoners flocked to as a place of mourning. In modern times the Cathedral is home to some of the most prestigious and high profile weddings and funerals that take place within the United Kingdom. If you have a penchant for the macabre, it is possible to purchase a sightseeing ticket which allows you to explore the Crypts which contain the bodies of Admiral Lord Nelson, Sir Christopher Wren and the Duke of Wellington. A sightseeing ticket will also give you access to the walkway which runs around the inside edge of the Cathedral's iconic dome, known as the Whispering Gallery due to its amazing acoustics allowing a whisper to be heard from the other side of the dome! If you have a head for heights, a sightseeing ticket also allow visitors to venture even further up to the Stone and Golden galleries which offer stunning views of London. St Paul's

Cathedral features many stunning design features, for example the incredible geometric staircase that looks remarkably similar to the shell of a giant snail. There are several different types of tours and sightseeing tickets available within St Paul's Cathedral. If you pay for a general ticket of admission you'll be treated to a 20 minuet introductory talk before being guided around the Cathedral's sights – this tour last for around 90 minutes and is available Monday to Saturday, 10am to 2pm. There is also a lot to enjoy for free! Services run throughout the week and are free to attend, as are the Choral Evensong sessions – which run on Monday to Saturday at 5pm, and on Sundays at 3:15pm. St Paul's Cathedral also has amazingly up kept, beautiful and expansive grounds that many visitors love to spend time exploring. Despite being situated in busy central London, the Cathedral's grounds always seem peaceful. We highly recommended visiting this architectural master piece as it is a true piece of London history.

Price

The standard sightseeing ticket will cost £18 for adults, £16 for students and £8 for under 18s. It is worth noting that you will be offered a discount if you purchase your tickets online. It is also possible to purchase family tickets which cost £44!

Location

St Paul's Churchyard, EC4M 8AD

20. THE LONDON DUNGEONS

If you have a morbid desire to immerse yourself within London's macabre history of murder, torture and other devious deeds then the London Dungeons is truly for you. The Dungeons explore, and bring to life, London's horrible past in a scary but also comedic style. The London Dungeons spent 40 years located under the railway arches on Tooley Street but has now moved to its new home on the South Bank. Despite the new location only being open since 2013, as you walk through the dingy, dark and cobbled alleyway entrance to the London Dungeons you will be surrounded by the smell of real, caged, rats which makes it hard to believe that the venue hasn't been scaring customers for centuries! The Dungeon offers an immersive 90 minuet tour which takes you through a living museum. Visitors will head recounts of horrendous historical stories, about London's past, which are told and performed by an amazingly talented cast of period costumed actors. Alongside the cast, there are a plethora of smells, props, rides and atmospheric lighting to help fully engage and immerse the visitors in the tales of plague-ridden houses, evil kings, torture, murder and terror. The costuming and makeup is truly first class – especially the disgusting puss filled boils present on most of the peasants! Some of the themes explored within the tour are: the tale and mystery surrounding the infamous Jack the Ripper, the Gunpowder Plot and Guy Fawkes, the executions of his wives and traitors performed by Henry VIII and much much more. There is no age limit for the tour, however it is recommended for ages 12-plus as there are multiple costumed jump scares! The tour allows anyone to drop out at key points if they are feeling overly scared or queasy from all the smells and costumes. If you are fascinated by the macabre and spooky – the London Dungeons is a perfect addition to your trip to London!

Price

A ticket for a tour of the London Dungeons costs £30 for adults and £24 for children under the age of 15. It is important to note that you can save up to £8 if you book online.

Location

County Hall, Westminster Bridge Rd, SE1 7PB

21.KENSINGTON PALACE

Kensington Palace is one of London's many palaces and is a location where hundreds of years of incredible British events have taken place. Kensington Palace has been the home of Henry VIII and is also the place where Anne Boleyn nearly had her head cut off! Kensington Palace has house some of the most popular British princesses of modern times! Visitors will be able to explore the rooms that Victoria stayed in before she was promoted to Queen. Princess Margaret and Princess Diana spent years living in the Palace. After Princess Diana's death, Kensington Palace's golden gates became the focal point of the thousands of flowers and cards of tribute sent by the grieving public. Both Princess Diana and Princess Margaret were considered to be fashionistas in their time and would often heavily influence the popular trends within the United Kingdom. Due to this Kensington Palace has become the royal residence most associated with fashion, glamour and style. The Palace houses an exhibition known as 'Diana: Her Fashion Story,' which showcases all of her most famous pieces of clothing including the velvet gown she wore when she danced with Jon Travolta at the White House. The Palace's interior is as decadent as its fashionable reputation. When George I ascended to the throne he had the whole Palace lavishly decorated. The private royal apartment, the Queens' State Apartment and the Palace's ground are all part of the guided tour. The Palace also offers a 'Digital Mission' which are interactive routes around the Palace, powered by an app. A tour around Kensington Palace is a truly unique insight into the life and history of British royalty.

Price

A tour around Kensington Palace costs £18 for adults, £14.30 for students and is free for anyone under the age of 16. It is important to note that you can get a slight discount by booking in advance online.

Location

The Broadwalk, Kensington Gardens, W8 4PX

22. THE SKY GARDEN

The Sky Garden is located on Fenchurch Street, in the very center of the City. This beautiful venue cause a media fanfare during its launch back in 2015 and it remains one of London's most popular attractions. The Sky Garden is located on the 35th floor, which makes it one of London's highest up gardens, to experience some truly spectacular views. The Sky Garden has boasts three floors of landscaped gardens which are flush with luscious South African and Mediterranean plants. There are also multiple observation decks, an open-air terrace, two restaurants, a rather expensive bar and an uninterrupted panoramic view of London's skyline. While entry to the Sky Garden is free, visitors must book their 90 minuet timeslot at least three days in advance of this visit date. Sky Garden is definitely one of London's best romantic spots as the view of the city at twilight is truly the perfect backdrop to any date. We highly recommended checking out the Sky Garden for nothing more than its spectacular, and free, view!

Price

Entry to the Sky Garden is completely free. However food and drinks from the cafes, bars and restaurants will have their own premiums.

Location

1 Sky Garden Walk, 20 Fenchurch St, EC3M 8AF

23. LONDON TRANSPORT MUSEUM

The London Transport Museum is perfect for anyone who has an interest in the transportation systems that are operational in London and transportation generally. The entrance of the Museum boasts an audiovisual recording of the most interesting transportation systems in the world and includes footage from: New York, Tokyo, Paris, New Delhi, Shanghai and of course London. The Museum house many interesting replicas of traditional London transport such as the capital's first licensed public transport the Sedan chair. There is also a replica of the horse drawn omnibuses that were common place on the streets of London in the early 1800s. There is also a very interesting exhibition that contains a recreation of London's first passenger railway – with is the train line from London Bridge to Greenwich which was constructed in 1833. The first floor contains potentially the most interesting displays which include the first underground engine (which was steam powered), a wooden Metropolitan Railway coach and an example of modern technology that is still used on the Tube today! There is also a large collection of Frank Pick's design work. Pick was the man behind the iconic underground signage which has become an iconic visualization of commuter life in London. There is also an example of the first every underground map which was produced by Harry Beck. The Museum is incredibly family friendly and offers a play zone for children under the age of seven. The Baby DLR features an interactive wall and building blocks to help keep small infants entertained. We highly recommended visiting the London Transport Museum as it offers a truly unique insight to how London implemented transportation and travel, which unarguably aided the city's economic growth.

Price

A ticket of admission to the London Transport Museum will cost £16 for adults and £13.50 for anyone under the age of 18.

Location

Covent Garden Piazza, WC2E 7BB

24. BUCKINGHAM PALACE

Buckingham Palace is a must visit for anyone visiting London for the first time. Buckingham Palace is the home of the Queen of England and the building's ground and architecture are a true reflection of the prestige surrounding the British monarchy. Buckingham Palace is in a perfect location as it is a short distance from the Houses of Parliament and is also surrounded by beautiful parkland. Queen Victoria requested a large balcony be constructed to allow her to send off and welcome back her troops. The balcony is now also where the Royal Family stands, and waves, during occasions of national interest and importance. One interesting event that recently occurred at Buckingham Palace was when the Queen was collected and escorted to her helicopter, by James Bond, before she was dropped off into the Olympic Stadium in 2012. Buckingham Palace is the working headquarters of the British Monarchy and both daily meetings and large scale ceremonies take place there. The Queen and the Duke of Edinburgh live in a private section of the Palace but there is still a large amount of the Palace able to be viewed by the public. The Queen's Gallery is open all year round, the Royal Mews are open from February to November, and the State Rooms are accessible to visitors throughout August and September. There are also more in-depth tours available on specific dates throughout the year – these tours are dependent on the Queen being out of the Palace and thus are unpredictable and vary on a yearly basis. It is important to note that if the Royal Standard flag is flying atop Buckingham Palace it means the Queen is in residence – otherwise a standard Union Jack flag will be flown. Visiting Buckingham Palace is a must as it gives a perfect example of the prestigious past of the United Kingdom.

Price

Prices vary massively! A tour of Buckingham Palace that includes the changing of the guard ceremony will cost roughly £75 per head. A tour of Buckingham Palace which includes afternoon tea will cost roughly £120. We recommended searching for offers online!

Location

Buckingham Palace Rd, SW1A 1AA

25. NATIONAL GALLERY

The National Gallery was established in 1824 as a new art collection created for the purpose of entertaining and educating the masses. Originally the National Gallery consisted of only 38 pictures which were displayed at a house in Pall Mall while a purpose built gallery was constructed! The construction of the National Gallery's new building was completed in 1838 and it was situated in Trafalgar Square, which was at the time considered to be the heart of London. Trafalgar Square was deemed the best location as it allowed poor people to visit the gallery by foot and richer people to attend the gallery from the west end via carriage. The National Gallery now hold over 2,3000 works of art and includes everything from medieval classic to world-famous pieces by French Impressionist. The National Gallery has stayed true to its roots and is free to visit. The gallery has blockbuster exhibitions, music, concerts and courses in traditional and modern artistic techniques. There are also multiple free lectures that are held each day – seats to which are based upon a first come first serve basis. The lectures take a closer look at the different paintings, artistic movements and artistic themes. The National Gallery some of the world's most famous paintings such as Vann Gogh's 'Sunflowers,' JMW Turner's 'Bequest' and Cezanne's 'Bathers.' The gallery also offers a plethora of activities for children ages between 5 and 12 which run throughout the year – with an increase in activity during the summer holidays. These activities give children a chance to explore the gallery while also taking part in first hand drawing, painting and artistic workshops. Like everything else in the National Gallery, these workshops for children are free and based on a first come first serve basis. Due to its high amount of cultural content exhibited at the National Gallery and its lack of entry price, we highly recommended checking it out on your visit to London.

Price

Entry to the National Gallery is free. All the lectures and workshops held at the Gallery are likewise free.

Location

Trafalgar Square, WC2N 5DN

26. LONDON WETLAND CENTRE

The London Wetland Centre is a huge 105 acre expanse of city wildlife area which was created by the Wildfowl and Wetlands Trust in the early 2000s. The four disused Victorian made reservoirs, which are located in the middle of the Thames, have been softened by extensive landscaping and weathered by nature to become an extensive landscape of lagoon, islets and pastures. Visitors can explore the entire of the beautiful wetlands, without getting wet or mucky, by traversing large glass enclosed walkways. At intervals alone the peaceful walkways there are multiple hiding spots that allow visitors to perch on a bench and look out at the wildlife that makes the wetlands their home. It is commonplace to be able to spot kingfishers, falcons, herons, sandmartins and sparrowhawks! The Wetland Centre also offers a wide range of exhibitions to educate visitors on the wildlife present within the wetlands and the reasons why there is such a need for the wetlands to be present within a city like London. The Centre also offers guides walking tours for those who want to learn more about the wildlife, birdlife and the flora. During the day there are also wildlife photography courses, pond-dipping sessions and many other day activities. At night there are also bat-spotting walks! The London Wetland Centre also has a lovely café that was a large outdoor terrace that overlooks the wetlands. If you have a hankering for wildlife exploration in heart of the United Kingdom's busiest metropolis then the London Wetland Centre is truly for you!

Price

A ticket of admission to the London Wetland Centre will cost £12.35 for adults, £9.20 for students and £6.90 for children under the age of 17. There is also a family ticket available for £34.50. Courses cost an additional premium.

Location

Queen Elizabeth's Walk, SW1 9WT

27.LONDON ZOO

London Zoo has been drawing huge crowds of tourists for nearly 200 years! It is estimated that over 1.5 million people visit the London Zoo on a yearly basis – which makes it one of London's most popular attractions! One of the Zoo's most interesting historical moment is when Charles Darwin was made a fellow to the Zoo in 1837. The Zoo is home to nearly 20,000 animals from over 800 species which is why it is necessary for the Zoo to span over 36 acres! London Zoo is opens every day of the year at 10am – except for Christmas Day – which means that you will definitely be able to incorporate it into your visit to London. The Zoo's closing time is dependent on the season: 6pm during summer, 5:30 during autumn, 4:30during winter and 5:30 during spring. One of the Zoo's main attractions is the Gorilla Kingdom. The Gorilla Kingdom was constructed over a period of 18 months in the early 2000s. The Gorilla Kingdom allows customers to view gorillas at play in their outside enclosure and watch them relax in their inside Plexiglas gym. If you want to see the gorillas up close we recommend visiting the Gorilla Kingdom later on in the day, as when its cooler, the gorillas move inside. Another main attraction is the Penguin Beach which is home to over 60 African, Rockhopper and Humboldt penguins. The Penguin Beach is surrounded by a large amphitheater which provides pool side views of the penguins at play. We recommended visiting Penguin Beach during feeding times as this is when the penguins are most playful and active! If you are interested in where the penguins used to be house you can visit the Grade I which was created in the 1930s and is a true testament to early modernist architecture. Other attractions of note are the Rainforest Life exhibition, the Komodo Dragon enclosure and the public aquarium. London Zoo is the perfect place to spend a day exploring and learning about the different animals found in this amazing zoo!

Price

The price of a ticket of admission to London Zoo is based upon the season. During the summer season a ticket of admission will cost an adult £25 and a child £19. During autumn, winter and spring entry will be £1-£2 cheaper.

Location

London Zoo, NW1 4RY

28.FREUD MUSEUM

The Freud Museum is situated in the house that Sigmund Freud made his home after he fled the Nazis in 1938. The Museum is preserved as a time capsule – a small chunk of 1930s Hapsburg Vienna transported to London's Hampstead. The museum contains the couch in which psychoanalysis was created and tested! Freud's study and library include an extensive collection of books on psychology, science and philosophy. The library also has multiple Egyptian, Greek and Roman antiques! The top floor of the museum is dedicated to Freud daughter, Anna, who also practiced psychoanalysis in the house until her death in 1982. The Freud Museum is one of the few museums in London to have two blue plaques, one for Sigmund and one for Anna. The museum offers an exhibition of films, which were taken in the 1930s, that depict the Freud family at home, in the garden and walking their dogs.

Price

A ticket of admission to the Freud Museum will cost £7 for an adult, £4 for school children and £5 for university students. Children under the age of 12 can enter the museum for free.

Location

20 Maresfield Gardens, NW3 5SX

29. WIMBLEDON LAWN TENNIS MUSEUM

The Wimbledon Lawn Tennis Museum is the easiest way to gain an insight into both Wimbledon's and the game of tennis' history. Despite being based on a sport that is known for its strict adherence to tradition, the Wimbledon Lawn Tennis Museum is surprisingly futuristic. The Museum includes a huge 3D cinema that explains the science behind the game and broadcasts interviews with both current and retired players. An interactive area allows visitors to handle different models of racquets – this truly lets visitors understand how far the sport has progressed since its inception! The interactive area also has replica trophies to let visitors feel their weight and take photos. There is also a surreal holographic 'ghost' of former tennis world champion John McEnroe which roams the dressing rooms. This 'ghost' catches many visitors off guard and more often than not causes a spectacle!! The Museum holds memorabilia that dates back as the 1550s and also includes modern memorabilia such as Andy Murray's outfit from the London 2012 Olympic games, where he took home the gold medal. There is also a series of tennis posters that date from the 1890s to 2015 – this again shows how far the sport and advertising has come! The Museum also offer behind the scenes tours of the grounds and facilities – including Centre Court – which allows visitors to get a 360 degree view of the arena from a special viewing platform. If you have an interest in tennis or sporting history, the Wimbledon Lawn Tennis Museum is a must visit!

Price

Prices vary depending on the season in which you visit. A ticket for an adult will normally cost between £13 and £24 while a ticket for a child (16 and under) will normally cost between £8 and £15.

Location

Church Rd, SW19 5AE

30.WARNER BROS. STUDIO TOUR LONDON – THE MAKING OF HARRY POTTER

Visit the studios who produced the incredibly popular Harry Potter movies, step into Hogwarts, explore Diagon Alley and drink a flagon of butterbeer. For over ten years, the warehouses and film lot at Laverden, were the base of operation for the Harry Potter movie series. Apart from on-location scenes, the majority of the filming was done here and as the movies came to completion Warner Bros. redeveloped, expanded and enhanced the facilities to enable the public tour and explore how the films were made. JK Rowling's original stories were still being published while the first few films were being produced – which meant that every set, prop, costume and construction was carefully crafted and stored in case they would be needed for a future film. As a result, the workshops, store rooms and film sets forma an incredibly extensive collection of Harry Potter artifacts that would enchant any avid Potterhead. The Making of Harry Potter is no ordinary tour as it lets visitors explore the Great Hall of Hogwarts, Diagon Alley, Platform 9¾ (which is complete with a huge originally steam engine that pulled the Hogwarts Express during filming), Dumbledore's office and many other incredible sets! The tour is the perfect place to learn more about the artistry of the production – the special effects, the animatronics and the methods the film crew used to bring the wonderful cast to life! The site also includes a gift shop that allows visitors to purchase flagons of butterbeer and their own wands – you can also purchase replicas of the main character's wands. If you are interested in film production or Harry Potter, the Warner Bro. Studio Tour London The Making Of Harry Potter is a perfect day trip for you!

Price

A ticket of admission costs £35 for an adult, £27 for a child ages between 5-15 and £107 for a family ticket.

Location

Studio Tour Drive, Leavesden, WD25 7LR

TRAVELERS WARNING

This section is a brief outline of things to do and things to avoid for ANY holiday! Before going on holiday it is considered best practice to make sure that your home is secure and to inform family, or friends, as to where you will be going and how long you will be gone for. This allows people to have an expectation of when you will be back and will also allow them to inform the correct authorities of your last known location in case of an emergency. It is also advisable to change your money into local currency before you start your holiday if you are traveling abroad as it is often cheaper. It is also advisable to notify your bank that you will be on holiday and may be making irregular purchases on your Debit/Credit cards. If you are traveling with expensive, or easily damaged, luggage it may also be worth considering purchasing travel insurance. We also suggest that you do not wear or display overtly expensive belongings during your trip – unless you are comfortable doing so. It is ALWAYS better to be safe than sorry!

Printed in Great Britain
by Amazon

12487140R00048